HIP-HOP

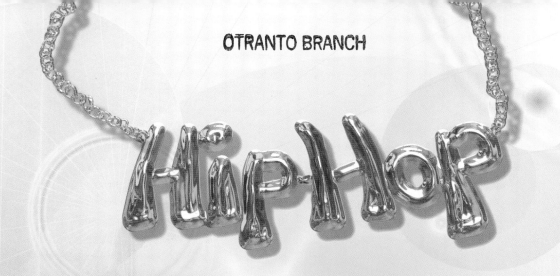

Hip-Hop

Reverend Run (Run-D.M.C.)

Terrell Brown

Mason Crest Publishers

Reverend Run (Run-D.M.C.)

FRONTIS Reverend Run has traveled a sometimes-rough path toward happiness and success as a minister and rapper.

PRODUCED BY 21ST CENTURY PUBLISHING AND COMMUNICATIONS, INC.

EDITORIAL BY HARDING HOUSE PUBLISHING SERVICES, INC.

MASON CREST PUBLISHERS INC.
370 Reed Road
Broomall, Pennsylvania 19008
(866)MCP-BOOK (toll free)
www.masoncrest.com

Printed in Malaysia.

First Printing

9 8 7 6 5 4 3 2 1

Library of Congress Cataloging-in-Publication Data

Brown, Terrell.
    Reverend Run / by Terrell Brown.
      p. cm. — (Hip-hop)
    Includes bibliographical references and index.
    ISBN 1-4222-0127-9 (alk. paper)
    1. Simmons, Joseph—Juvenile literature. 2. Run-D.M.C. (Musical group)—
Juvenile literature. 3. Rap musicians—United States—Biography—Juvenile
literature. 4. Clergy—United States—Biography—Juvenile literature.
I. Title. II. Series.
ML3930.S547B76 2007
782.421649092—dc22
[B]   2006010879

Publisher's notes:
- All quotations in this book come from original sources, and contain the spelling and grammatical inconsistencies of the original text.

- The Web sites mentioned in this book were active at the time of publication. The publisher is not responsible for Web sites that have changed their addresses or discontinued operation since the date of publication. The publisher will review and update the Web site addresses each time the book is reprinted.

Contents

Hip-Hop Timeline

1974 Hip-hop pioneer Afrika Bambaataa organizes the Universal Zulu Nation.

1988 *Yo! MTV Raps* premieres on MTV.

1970s Hip-hop as a cultural movement begins in the Bronx, New York City.

1985 *Krush Groove*, a hip-hop film about Def Jam Recordings, is released featuring Run-D.M.C., Kurtis Blow, LL Cool J, and the Beastie Boys.

1970s DJ Kool Herc pioneers the use of breaks, isolations, and repeats using two turntables.

1979 The Sugarhill Gang's song "Rapper's Delight" is the first hip-hop single to go gold.

1986 Run-D.M.C. are the first rappers to appear on the cover of *Rolling Stone* magazine.

1970   1980   1988

1976 Grandmaster Flash & the Furious Five pioneer hip-hop MCing and freestyle battles.

1986 Beastie Boys' album *Licensed to Ill* is released and becomes the best-selling rap album of the 1980s.

1970s Break dancing emerges at parties and in public places in New York City.

1982 Afrika Bambaataa embarks on the first European hip-hop tour.

1988 Hip-hop music annual record sales reaches $100 million.

1970s Graffiti artist Vic pioneers tagging on subway trains in New York City.

1984 *Graffiti Rock*, the first hip-hop television program, premieres.

1993 Rapper Snoop Dogg's album *Doggystyle* is the first debut album to hit the music charts at number one.

2006 Queen Latifah becomes the first hip-hop artist to receive a star on the Hollywood Walk of Fame.

1989 DJ Jazzy Jeff & The Fresh Prince become the first hip-hop artists to win a Grammy Award.

2003 Rapper Eminem becomes the first hip-hop artist to win an Academy Award.

2005 Hip-hop artist Kanye West appears on the cover of *Time* magazine.

1989 Rap is added as a new category to the *Billboard* charts.

1997 East Coast rapper Notorious B.I.G. (aka Biggie Smalls) is murdered.

2004 First National Hip-Hop Political Convention is held in Newark, New Jersey.

1989   **2000**   **2006**

1996 West Coast rapper Tupac Shakur is shot and killed.

2005 Rapper Will Smith opens the Philadelphia Live 8 concert as part of 10 simultaneous concerts held worldwide to bring attention to the extreme poverty in Africa.

1990s Hip-hop emerges in Europe.

1989 First gangsta rap album, *Straight Outta Compton*, is released by N.W.A.

2001 The hip-hop political action group, Hip-Hop Summit Action Network, is founded by Russell Simmons.

1992 Dr. Dre's album *The Chronic* is released; it redefines West Coast rap.

2006 The Smithsonian Institute National Museum of American History announces the creation of a new hip-hop exhibition scheduled to open in three to five years.

Rappers Run-D.M.C. were winners at the first *Soul Train* Music Awards, taking home honors in two categories. Shown here in this 1988 photo are (left to right) Joseph "Run" Simmons, Darryl "D.M.C." McDaniels, and Jason "Jam-Master Jay" Mizell.

◄ 1 ►

Soul Train

Back in 1987, all the shining stars of the African American music world were at the televised First Annual *Soul Train* Music Awards. Dionne Warwick was there, and so were Whitney Houston, Janet Jackson, Grace Jones, Stevie Wonder, and Barry White. A new up-and-coming rap group was there as well, Run-D.M.C.

Producer Don Cornelius had started *Soul Train* in 1971 as the first African American variety show. It was a way for black musicians to get their music on television, where people could hear it, and record sales shot up as a result. The *Soul Train* Music Awards was a way to further that goal. These television shows were truly a train that carried black Americans' voices to the entire country.

At the end of that evening back in 1987, Run-D.M.C. went home with two awards. For Joseph Simmons, one of the group's members, it was a fantasy come alive. It proved to him that dreams really do come true. Years later, he wrote in his **memoir**, a book called *It's Like That*:

> **"One of the most powerful things you can do is have faith in yourself. Dreams are real and can happen, but it all starts with believing in yourself.**
>
> **When I was growing up I had this dream of becoming somebody famous. I didn't know what I would do, but I continued to dream and work hard. Then I got into rapping and my whole life changed.**
>
> **People would say negative things, but I just kept believing in myself. It didn't happen overnight, but it did happen."**

How It Happened

Joseph Simmons, who would one day be known as "Run," was born on November 14, 1964. For the first years of his life, his family, including his older brothers Russell and Daniel Jr., called him Joey. Their father was a college professor, who taught Joey a love for words.

The family lived in Hollis, Queens, a solid, middle-income neighborhood that nevertheless felt the strong influence of another nearby neighborhood, the Bronx. As Joey was growing up in Queens, not far away, a new culture called hip-hop was also growing up in the rough, bleak streets of the South Bronx.

Hip-Hop

Hip-hop included music, art, dance, speech, and fashion. In some ways, it was brand new—but in others, it was as ancient as Africa. Rap—hip-hop's rhyming, rhythmic music—has its roots deep in African culture and oral tradition. The earliest African Americans kept on listening to the echo of their homeland, and whether they were worshipping or working, they would play with words, using rhyme and rhythm to express themselves. These earliest forms of rap might have been called **testifying**, schoolyard rhymes, jailhouse rhymes, and jump-rope rhymes, but they were all African Americans getting together to rap.

Modern-day rap music came to life in the early 1970s, when a Jamaican **DJ** known as Kool Herc tried to use his Jamaican style of DJing—which involved reciting **improvised** rhymes over **dubbed**

As a young child working with older brother Russell and his rap clients, Joey became a skilled DJ with lightning-fast hands and constant chatter. Eventually, his talents would give him a nickname that put the Run in Run-D.M.C.

Hip-hop pioneer DJ Kool Herc originated break-beat DJing in the Bronx, New York City. Hip-hop has come a long way since those underground days of the early 1970s. In 2006, Kool Herc addressed a press conference announcing the first Hip-Hop Exhibition at the Smithsonian National Museum of American History.

versions of his **reggae** records—at parties in the Bronx of New York City. New Yorkers weren't into reggae back then, though, so Kool Herc adapted his style by chanting over the instrumental or percussion sections of the day's popular songs. Because these instrumental and percussion breaks were relatively short, he learned to extend them indefinitely by using an audio **mixer** and two identical records to continuously replay the desired segment. Rap took off from there.

The hip-hop culture—which also included graffiti street art and break dancing—caught on so quickly because it offered young urban New Yorkers a chance to express themselves. Rap was an art form anyone could do. You didn't need a lot of money or expensive instruments to rhyme. You didn't need to take lessons. Rapping could be practiced to perfection any time, anywhere.

Hip-hop gave kids growing up in the streets something they didn't have a whole lot of: hope. At a time when prejudice, poverty, and unemployment were the realities that ruled the inner city, hip-hop offered urban young people a way to excel. If they wanted to rap, they didn't have to follow a set of rules imposed on them by white authorities; the only rules they had to follow were to be original and rhyme on time to the beat of the music. Anything was possible. You could make up a rap about your girlfriend or your own skill or the man in the moon; it didn't matter. If you were laid back, you could rap at a slow pace. If you were a fast, jumpy sort of guy, you could rap at a fast pace. No two people rapped the same, even when reciting the same rhyme. Slow or fast, the smoother you rapped, the more praise you gathered, until you became an urban hero, with the same prestige as all the other urban heroes, sports stars, tough guys, and comedians—and rappers.

Back in the 1970s, rap was like a magnet to the kids on the streets, sucking them into its boom and its beat. Today, rap is still a form of self-expression that's within urban kids' reach—and it still gets them the **affirmation** from their peers for which all adolescents yearn. By the twenty-first century, however, hip-hop was a whole lot more than just something street kids were doing; it had also grown into a multi-million-dollar business. At the same time, it was still doing what African American music has always done—speaking out on behalf of the black community's political, social, and economic conditions.

But back when Joey Simmons first heard rap, it was just getting started.

Rhyming and Scratching

Joey may not have been born in the Bronx, and his family wasn't all that poor—but he knew about hip-hop. He wrote in his memoir:

"I never could have guessed that I would end up a rap star when I was growing up because there was

no such thing back then. Hip-hop was something that happened on the playgrounds, in parks and at parties. There was no big money. . . . There was nothing but guys on street corners and in alleys beating on trash cans or whatever they could find."

When Joey was twelve years old, he was given a drumset, and soon after that he got a turntable. He and his friends—D.M.C. (Darryl McDaniels), Butter Love, Runny Ray, and Terrible T—spent as much time as they could in D.M.C.'s basement, rhyming and making beats. They used D.M.C.'s mother's stereo system, and they bought themselves a mixer. They didn't have a lot of records to work with, but that didn't stop Joey from learning to scratch. They weren't thinking about growing up to become famous and make lots of money; they were just having fun. At this point, rap hadn't made it into stores yet anyway; it was still mostly just something friends did when they hung out together.

Every day, Joey went to school, came home, shot a few hoops, and then got together with his friends for some rhyming. The five boys called themselves the Hollis Crew. Butter Love and Joey were the group's clowns, the ones who always made the others laugh. Joey knew he could count on his friends to back him up and appreciate him for himself. His friendship with the Hollis Crew became a platform where he could build his self-esteem and confidence, a sort of launching pad where he could start his climb toward the sky.

Meanwhile, Joey's older brother Russell was getting into the management end of the business, promoting and booking gigs for rappers. Russell made friends with one of rap's big names, Kurtis Blow, and Kurtis was often a guest at the Simmons home. When Kurtis heard Joey rapping, he took the time to give him some pointers.

Kurtis Blow was a serious rapper who taught Joey about hip-hop's hard, street core—and Joey worked hard to imitate Kurtis's style. Kurtis rewarded Joey's efforts by making him his DJ. Joey started performing under the name Son of Kurtis Blow. He was still only twelve years old, but he was already making himself a name in the hip-hop world.

When Kurtis taught Joey how to rap and spin, he was teaching the genuine article: the *real* hip-hop that had come up out of the Bronx streets. The Sugarhill Gang had brought hip-hop to the world; they had

Run and D.M.C. (shown here) have been friends since childhood. Together with three other friends, the Hollis Crew spent many hours in D.M.C.'s basement, working out their sound using his mom's stereo, a mixer, and only a few records.

Kurtis Blow helped bring rap into the mainstream. He also taught Run about rap's roots. In 1979, Kurtis recorded *Christmas Rapping*, with Run as his DJ. Though Run didn't get credit for his work, he got something more important for his career—experience.

made it commercial, a hot new product. But Kurtis Blow and others like him had a different angle. They wanted to keep hip-hop real, true to its roots. From Kurtis, Joey learned that real hip-hop wasn't about being successful, getting famous, or making money. Instead, it was about staying true to the streets, the black community that had endured so much over the centuries. Hip-hop's guts were angry and honest and brave—and rappers belted out those guts where everyone could see and hear. That's what Joey wanted for his sound.

As a DJ, Joey's hands could fly. His speed earned him the name of Run; he was the **epitome** of hurry, the embodiment of hustle. According to his older brother Russell, "He could literally cut the air."

The first record Joey helped make was way back then, with Kurtis Blow, a record called *Christmas Rapping*. Although Joey was never credited, he wrote most of the second half of the album. He didn't gain any fame for his work—but he did gain experience.

A New Name

One spring afternoon, Russell and a friend were barbecuing in the Simmons's backyard, while twelve-year-old Joey chattered on and on to them, running his mouth like there was no tomorrow. "DJ Run!" the friend laughed.

"It was the coolest thing I had ever heard," Run wrote later. "Now I had a new identity. I was DJ Run, sorta like Superman or Spawn, the new superhero, only nobody knew it yet."

DJ Run was on his way to being a soul train superhero, someone who spoke out brave and strong on behalf of the African American community. He had a hard-core urban attitude, but he was different from the rest: he had something important to say, and the courage and honesty to say it loud. Before long, people would find out what a superhero he really was.

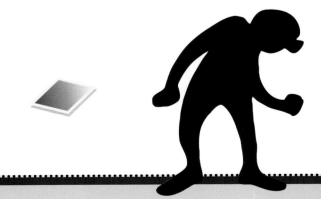

Rolling Stone

ISSUE NO. 488 · DECEMBER 4TH, 1986 · U.K. £1.90 · $1.95

RUN-D.M.C.
Sets the Record Straight on Rap Music and Violence

WHEEL OF FORTUNE
Why 42 Million Americans Need It Every Day

WHAT IT'S LIKE TO BE YOUNG IN SOUTH AFRICA

THE TALK-SHOW EPIDEMIC

WILLIAM GREIDER ON REAGAN'S STAR WARS FANTASY

SID & NANCY A PUNK TRAGEDY

When Jam-Master Jay came on board, Run and D.M.C. were ready to hit the big time. And they did, in 1986 becoming the first rap group featured on the cover of *Rolling Stone* magazine, a sure sign the trio had arrived.

2

Run's House

Run and Darryl McDaniels ended up going to different high schools, but that didn't stop their friendship from growing as the years went by. Darryl liked drawing, and Run liked basketball, but the two boys shared their rap dreams. They were as close as brothers—and they were starting to dream big.

The two friends performed off and on at an underage club in Hollis. When they went off to college—Run to LaGuardia Community College and Darryl to St. John's University—they kept in touch. Pretty soon, they brought a third member into their group, Jason Mizell, known as Jam-Master Jay.

The Birth of Run-D.M.C.

Although Russell Simmons was excited about his little brother's talent, he wasn't too sure what he thought about D.M.C. Russell was ready to lay the foundations for his brother's solo career, but Run was loyal to his friend. "If I can't be down with Dee," he told Russell, "I really don't want to make records." So Russell gave in, and the two boys practiced in the Simmons living room, developing a style all their own. Run would start a rhyme, and Darryl would finish it.

Pretty soon they moved out of the living room. At first, they performed for free in the parks and at parties around New York. But then Russell found them gigs further and further from home, and by the time they were eighteen, they were playing in places like Wisconsin and North Carolina, places that had never heard of rap music until they heard Run and D.M.C. doing their thing.

Before long, they were making money on their gigs. Jam-Master Jay was their DJ, and the crowds were going crazy. Run-D.M.C. had been born.

Trendsetters

Run-D.M.C. built on the sound of the older classic rappers (people like Grandmaster Flash and Whodini) and came up with their own brand-new sound. The crowds loved their beats. In 1983, Russell produced their first single, "It's Like That/Sucker MC's"—and the song became an instant hit. Run-D.M.C.'s rapping was fun and yet serious. Their rhymes made people laugh, but they also made people think.

The band signed a record deal with Profile Records in 1983. Russell had just formed his own management company, Rush Productions, and he signed on Run-D.M.C. Then he got busy promoting his brother's group. Russell knew the guys had what it took to be big.

The way Run-D.M.C. dressed was just as fresh as their sound. They became famous for their baggy black sweat suits, their black Fedora hats, and their Adidas sneakers with no laces. Jam-Master Jay was the one responsible for their look.

It all got started back in 1984, when the three young men had just started making plenty of money. They were pulling in a couple of thousand dollars for every gig—and in a single night, they could fit in two shows in Brooklyn and two shows in Yonkers or Queens—which meant the money was rolling in. Jay wanted to show it off, so one day he went strolling down Jamaica Avenue, the main shopping drag in Queens, dressed in a black hat and a black leather coat, gold chains around his neck and designer sunglasses hiding his eyes. People were impressed.

Music wasn't the only way Run-D.M.C. influenced the hip-hop world. Even their clothing was unique among rap artists. In this 2002 photo, the group is seen arriving at the MTV Video Music Awards, wearing their characteristic black Fedora hats and black leather suits.

Russell was good at promotion, and he knew the cool look worked for the group. So he smoothed out pieces of their ensembles a little more—and then he made it famous. Before long, kids in cities across America wanted to dress like Run-D.M.C.

Living the Fantasy

For Run, life seemed like a dream. At twenty years old, he had already made it to the top. One night at a concert in Madison Square Garden in New York City, Run strolled across the stage and then shouted into the mike, "Whose house is it?"

The crowd went crazy. "Run's house!" they screamed.

Run wrote in his memoir:

> **"I remember looking out over the audience, feeling like I was on top of the world. I could see people every-where, all shades, rocking to the power of Run-D.M.C. . . . I was the king of rap, and it was like me and the crowd were one. . . . At the spur of the moment—things were at an all-time high—I had everyone in the whole Garden lift their sneakers in the air.**
>
> **The spotlight was racing across the crowd, and twenty thousand pairs of Adidas were raised."**

The Adidas company had never sold so many sneakers. No wonder a representative from the company offered Run-D.M.C. a $2 million deal to endorse its product line.

And all the while, Run-D.M.C.'s music was going strong. Run-D.M.C. was the first to create rap albums (instead of single songs only). Everything they said or did seemed enchanted, like gold was just dripping from their fingers all over their lives. Their first albums, *Run-D.M.C.*, *King of Rock*, and *Raising Hell*, were as successful as everything else they touched.

Run-D.M.C. was faithful to the old-style hip-hop sound—but they took it to places it had never been before. Before long, they had accumulated a whole string of "firsts":

- They were the first rap group nominated for a Grammy Award.

- They were the first rappers to be on the cover of *Rolling Stone* magazine.

- They were the first rappers to have an album go **gold** (*Run-D.M.C.* in 1984).

- They were the first rap group to have an album go **platinum** (*King of Rock* in 1985).

- They were the first rap group to earn a multi-platinum album (*Raising Hell* in 1986).

- They were the first rap group to combine rap with live, original metal guitar.

- They were the first rap group to have their videos played regularly on MTV.

- They were the first rappers to appear on *American Bandstand* and *Saturday Night Live.*

- They had the first rap song to reach the top ten on *Billboard*'s Hot 100 ("Walk This Way" in 1986, with Steven Tyler and Joe Perry of Aerosmith).

Run-D.M.C. brought rap to mainstream audiences and to the Grammys. They were the first rap group to be nominated for a Grammy Award, though they never won. Here, the three trailblazers are shown attending the Grammy Award ceremony in 1988.

The crew was no longer popular only with black city kids; young people across the entire country loved Run-D.M.C. Their performance at the famous 1985 Live Aid concert (which raised money for people starving in Ethiopia) added to their mainstream success. *Raising Hell* soon became the highest-selling rap album in history, reaching number three on the *Billboard* album charts and selling over 3 million copies.

It wasn't only their fans who loved Run-D.M.C.; they'd also gained the respect of other rappers. That respect brought them a new set of

In 1985, Run-D.M.C. joined such rappers as Kurtis Blow, LL Cool J, and the Beastie Boys in the film *Krush Groove*. The movie was a fictional version of the early days of Russell Simmons's Def Jam Records.

opportunities: they headlined with LL Cool J and Whodini; they appeared in *Krush Groove* with Kurtis Blow, the Beastie Boys, and the Fat Boys; and they recorded with Aerosmith's Steven Tyler and Joe Perry. This meant they had crossed the line between hip-hop and rock'n'roll. Now they were appealing to both rockers and rappers.

"Everything came in a whirlwind," Run wrote years later.

> **"Success flowed like water: television interviews, magazine covers, packed arenas from coast to coast. . . . I was feeling confident and strong, like I owned the world. I was truly the king of rap, setting trends, winning honors, and selling millions of albums."**

Things looked amazing for Run-D.M.C. But Run had gotten off track; he was no longer even sure where he was going. "Almost overnight, mad confusion set in and things began to change," Run wrote in his memoir.

> **"I bought new cars, Rolex watches—anything flashy that made me feel and look like the king of rap. The problem was I didn't have the money to fuel the lifestyle. I did anything to avoid facing the pain inside. But when your world is all about consumption, you're only going to consume yourself in the end."**

Something was not right in Run's house.

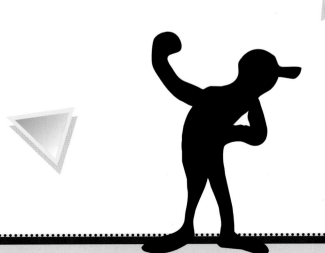

Run found out that success brought its own problems. In 1988, Run-D.M.C. released *Tougher Than Leather*, followed by a movie of the same name and a tour. All failed to live up to expectations. Neither did Run's life, and he knew he had to change.

3

Back from Hell

Run was using drugs. He was going out with a different woman every night. He was still rapping, and he thought he was having a good time. But the truth was, his life was getting more and more messed up. And then he started to get depressed.

Tougher Than Leather

Things weren't going so well for the rest of Run-D.M.C. either. In 1988, they made an album called *Tougher Than Leather*; they followed it up with a movie by the same name; and then they took it on the road for the Tougher Than Leather Tour. But at their shows, suddenly the arenas were only a little more than half full. The album wasn't selling well, and the movie was a flop.

Critics, however, liked the album *Tougher Than Leather*. According to Ira Robbins from Trouser Press:

"*Tougher Than Leather* is . . . a self-assured superstar record with a dense, rock-influenced sound that's become as distinguishable as the crew's trademark verbal jousting. . . . Throughout, the witty writing, deft delivery, and riotously crowded production make *Tougher Than Leather* a **progressive** and **peerless** statement of the art that neither excludes nor panders to any audience segment."

The album sampled classic rock records—everything from the Monkees' "Mary, Mary" to the Temptations' "Papa Was a Rollin' Stone," along with smaller bites from James Brown, Malcolm X, Led Zeppelin, and even old Run-D.M.C. themselves—creating a fresh, funny sound that played off the past while creating some new and all their own. The trio was proving that hip-hop was still the flexible, creative sound that could pull together rhythms and rhymes from everywhere and everything.

But the guys who had built the foundation for hip-hop were no longer competing with the newer pop-rap that was being built on what Run-D.M.C. had originally laid down. According to music critic Ira Robbins, those "soft-headed rappers weren't worthy of lacing the trio's Adidas"—but that didn't matter to the people buying the albums. The new rap was laced with sex and violence, while Run-D.M.C. tried to stay funny, clean, and inspirational. The group's refusal to give their fans what they wanted didn't sell albums. Suddenly, Run-D.M.C., the trendsetters, had turned into three has-beens.

Depression

Run felt more and more depressed. He and the rest of Run-D.M.C. went on tour with Public Enemy, Jazzy Jeff, and the Fresh Prince (Will Smith), but nothing was jiving for Run. He was so down that he started to think about killing himself. And meanwhile, the money was running out. In his memoir, he described this era of his life:

"When the movie and the album failed, our reign as kings began to end. After years of ruling supreme, it seemed that everything we touched was no longer turning to gold. We no longer were the men of the moment, no longer poster b-boys for the American Dream."

But things were going to get even worse.

Run D.M.C. loved to perform for their fans all across the country. In 1987, Run-D.M.C. and another very popular rap group, the Beastie Boys, announced their "Together Forever" tour. The groups (shown here after a press conference announcing the tour) would travel to forty cities.

Back from Hell

In 1991, after a Run-D.M.C. concert in Cleveland, Ohio, a woman from the audience accused Run of rape. Run ended up battling the charges in an Ohio courtroom. The legal fees cost him thousands of dollars—and there went all the money he had left. Eventually, the charges were dismissed, but Run's wife couldn't let him off the hook that easily.

Run may not have been guilty of rape, but his wife knew he wasn't being faithful to her. She packed up their kids and moved out of the home they shared. Soon after, she filed for divorce.

Run's life was in a shambles. He and his family were out of touch, and he had let a stream of publicists, managers, and fans replace his real friends. The people around him all seemed to want a little piece of Run—but there just wasn't enough to go around. Run no longer had time to shoot hoops; he no longer sat down for a family meal; and he no longer went to church. He had lost touch with all the things that kept him balanced.

A year earlier, in 1990, Run-D.M.C. released a new album, *Back from Hell*, a tough collection of mostly solo works that bore little resemblance to their earlier albums. This time around, they included plenty of swear words—but they kept their trademark power and intelligence. The album spoke directly (and sharply) to the black community about its social problems. The fans didn't like it, and by 1991, it was clear that *Back from Hell* was another flop.

Run's personal hell wasn't over yet, either. Around this time, Run and his brother Russell were going through a bad streak in their relationship. While Run's career was coming apart at the seams, Russell had started Def Jam Records and was already well on his way to being a hip-hop **mogul**. Run resented his brother's success; he felt Russell owed him, since Run-D.M.C.'s success had helped get Russell's business off the ground. Not until later did Run realize that "success is like sunlight. You don't have to hoard it. . . . We all can shine."

But back then in the 1990s, Run hadn't learned that yet. Run was starting to give his life some serious thought, though. Clearly, things weren't working out the way he had planned. Somewhere along the way, he had lost track of who he was. He wrote:

> **"Something had stolen my light, and I couldn't seem to get it back. It was then I started realizing that maybe I had been grabbing for the wrong things in life.**
>
> **The fame, money, and women weren't ending my depression or getting me closer to being Joey again. Or the real DJ Run.**
>
> **I got down on my knees and prayed. . . ."**

As Run thought and prayed, he started to change. It was a long, painful process, but he was finally taking the time to give his life serious consideration. He realized that the old Joey he had once been—the "real" Run—was like a diamond he had buried under dirt. This secret, genuine core was "the gift of God we all have within us whether we know it—or remember it—or not." Run explained in his memoir:

"Uncovering that diamond is the reinventing-yourself process. You first have to be able to see the new you in your mind's eye. . . . There's no way that you can bring about change in your life unless you can imagine and truly see yourself as you want to be.

As Run's life and career seemed to be on a downward spiral, his brother Russell's (left) seemed to soar to unbelievable heights. For a while, Run was jealous and resentful of Russell's accomplishments. After all, Run-D.M.C. had helped bring success to Def Jam Records.

> That is where prayer comes in. . . . Prayer is imagination; imagination is prayer. I totally believe that in my heart. God is inside you. . . . Prayer helps to shape your mind and aid you in visualizing what it is that you should be doing to uncover that diamond. **"**

Down with the King

At about this point in Run's life, he heard from one of his bodyguards about a church called Zoe Ministries in New York City. Run watched a televised service, and then he decided to pay a call on the pastor of the church, Bishop E. Bernard Jordan. When Bishop Jordan met Run, he told Run, "Get ready for a new life now!"

Run started going to Zoe Ministries every day. One day, he was seating people before a service when he noticed a teenage boy staring at him. Then he heard the boy whisper to the woman with him, "Grandma, that usher over there is Run-D.M.C." His grandmother hissed, "Shut up! All you think about is that rap music. Run-D.M.C. ain't no usher in a church!"

Plenty of people thought Run was strange for attending church all the time. But he didn't care. Life was starting to make sense to him for the first time. He quit using drugs. After a year and a half, he was serving the church as a **deacon**, and soon after that, he became "Reverend Run," an **ordained** minister. At first, people thought it was pretty funny that a rapper had turned into a reverend. Run didn't like the ridicule—but he didn't care enough to change. He felt his new name identified the new Joseph Simmons, the *real* Joseph Simmons, a rapper who served the Lord.

Run was no longer the king of his life; he had turned that role over to God. After everything he had been through, he had learned humility, as well as a lot of other important life lessons. But in lots of ways, he was still the same old Run. And rapping was as much a part of who he was as ever.

After three years with no new releases, Run-D.M.C. produced a comeback album, *Down with the King*. The album was a public announcement of Run's new faith, but at the same time it tied Run-D.M.C. to the group's past, their long history together starting back in Hollis, Queens. Run-D.M.C. was also trying to connect their old, classic hip-hop sound with the newer pop-hop. To do that, they

Run knew he had to find a better life path, and he did when he discovered Zoe Ministries. With the help and support of Bishop E. Bernard Jordan (right), Run quit using drugs and turned his life around. In 1995, Run became an ordained minister.

Run had his ups and his downs; he'd known success and failure. Treating his troubles as a learning experience, he wanted to share what he had learned and wrote down the lessons as something he called "house rules."

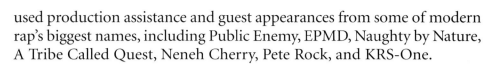

used production assistance and guest appearances from some of modern rap's biggest names, including Public Enemy, EPMD, Naughty by Nature, A Tribe Called Quest, Neneh Cherry, Pete Rock, and KRS-One.

Run's House Rule No. 1

Run had gone through some serious changes. His life had been knocked flat on its butt—but Run hadn't stayed on the ground. Instead, he'd picked himself up. He'd found himself again, the real Run who had gotten so off track, and he'd learned important lessons along the way. Down the road a ways, he'd write all these lessons down as "house rules" in his memoir. In his book, he explained the first of these rules: "You get what you put out."

❝You can't stay hot forever. What goes up will come down. No matter how big you get in the game, you will eventually come back down to earth. But remember, when the excitement and the celebrity eventually fade, you were a class act before it all began. Change is a natural state of being. It will happen, so be prepared. Stay humble and remember when things settle down to earth it's only part of life's natural process of regenerating itself. Like a flower blooming, something new has to grow. And remember, you reap what you sow. You get what you put out.❞

The members of Run-D.M.C. were moving on to other projects, but their importance to hip-hop was not forgotten. In February 2002, the trio was honored with their handprints on Hollywood's Rockwalk. Sadly, in October that same year, Jason "Jam-Master" Jay Mizell (left) was murdered.

4

End of
an Era

Run understood now that success has more than one definition—and he cared more about spiritual wealth than material riches. Darryl and Jay had also gone through some hard times—Darryl had struggled with alcoholism, and Jay had suffered through a bad car accident—but both men had also pulled their lives together and settled down.

Meanwhile, Run-D.M.C. had nearly reached the end of its road. They released another album, *Crown Royal*, that featured a crazy mix of guest artists—everyone from rappers Method Man, Nas, and Fat Joe, to rockers like Sugar Ray, Kid Rock, and Everlast—but the new CD met with little success. The crew joined Aerosmith and Kid Rock for a performance on MTV, and they went on tour with Aerosmith. But the three friends, Run, Darryl, and Jay, were putting most of their energy into other endeavors.

On February 25, 2002, Run, Darryl, and Jay, the three members of the group Run-DMC, were inducted into Hollywood's Rockwalk, in

In 2001, Method Man, Fat Joe, Everlast, and Kid Rock joined Run-D.M.C. on their album *Crown Royal*. Despite a tour, album sales were small, and after many years together, the end was in sight, though not the type of ending anyone would have wanted.

Los Angeles, California. Hollywood's Rockwalk is a sidewalk gallery dedicated to honoring artists who have made a significant contribution to the evolution of the music industry. Snoop Dogg, Jay-Z, Jermaine Dupri, and many other big names in the hip-hop world attended the event to show their respect for these three hip-hop pioneers.

And then everything came to an end for Run-D.M.C.

Murder

On October 30, 2002, while Jay was in a recording studio in Queens, he was shot in the head and killed. He was thirty-seven years old, and he left behind a wife and three children.

Because of Jay's professional association with hip-hop's rabble-rouser 50 Cent, the New York police focused on a possible revenge motive for the crime. Rumors circulated that organized crime was involved; others said that Jay was a casualty of an East Coast–West Coast war between rappers. As the investigation continued, various facts surfaced but few definite answers.

Federal agents eventually searched the offices of record label Murder Inc., looking for a connection with the crime. They found that Kenneth "Supreme" McGriff, a convicted drug dealer and a longtime friend of the Murder Inc. executives, had been plotting against 50 Cent as **retaliation** for a song 50 Cent had written about McGriff's criminal drug activities. According to the *New York Daily News,* Jam-Master Jay defied an industry **blacklist** of 50 Cent, thus earning McGriff's wrath.

Bottom line: Jay's death was a senseless killing. Run and Darryl were heartbroken. The week after Jay's death, they announced Run-D.M.C.'s official retirement. Nevertheless, Run still affirmed his faith. He told Contact Music:

> **"I loved him. We have more than one body and he's not dead—we're all eternal beings. Jay did what he was supposed to do. When it was done . . . he put his number two pencil down. Jam Master Jay has left the classroom. We're still here. I don't worry so much about why Jay has gone. I worry more about why I'm still here."**

Shortly before the murder, Run-D.M.C. had filmed a Dr. Pepper commercial with LL Cool J. When the commercial aired in 2002, it was the last public performance of Run-D.M.C. A dedication to Jam-Master Jay was added to the commercial's first airings.

Run and Darryl also helped organize a coalition of hip-hop musicians to create a fund for Jay's family. Rappers Sean "P. Diddy" Combs, Busta Rhymes, and Foxy Brown, as well as Run's brother, Russell Simmons, all showed up.

Jay's friends, including hip-hop greats like Big Daddy Kane and Funkmaster Flex, remembered him as one of hip-hop's pioneers and groundbreakers. Public Enemy paid tribute to him in a song. Jim Tremayne, editor of *DJ Times*, also acknowledged the importance of Jay's role within Run-D.M.C.: "People can't understand how important they were in pop music history. They were absolutely as revolutionary as Elvis," when it came to making rap popular—and it was Jay who provided the beat. Harry Allen of the *Village Voice* wrote that Jay would be remembered for "a personal style marked by deference and selflessness. . . . The supporting role he performed enabled him to act as a global ambassador for [hip-hop] in a manner absent of ego."

Hip-Hop and Violence: A Song of Hate?

Despite all the wonderful things being said about Jay, people were starting to question the connection between hip-hop and violence. Jay wasn't the first hip-hop artist to be murdered; Tupac Shakur and Biggie Smalls had also met violent deaths, as had others in the hip-hop community. A loud ugly rumble was growing across America: hip-hop was not only connected to violence, but it actually *caused* it.

Journalist John McWhorter in an article in *City Journal* described a scene he viewed while sitting in a fast-food restaurant in Harlem. Although it was 1:30 P.M. on a school day, eight black adolescents were having a food fight. They only stopped after a security guard threw them out of the restaurant. McWhorter wrote,

"These teens clearly weren't monsters, but they seemed to consider themselves exempt from public norms of behavior—as if they had begun to check out of mainstream society.

What struck me most, though, was how fully the boys' music—hard-edged rap, preaching bone-deep dislike of authority—provided them with a continuing soundtrack to their antisocial behavior. So completely was rap ingrained in their consciousness that every so often, one or another of them would break into cocky, expletive-laden rap lyrics, accompanied by the angular, bellicose gestures typical of rap performance. A couple of his buddies would then join him. Rap was a running decoration in their conversation."

Almost from its beginning, hip-hop had the reputation of being violent. But, the violence wasn't just in its lyrics; it extended to its people. Rapper Tupac Shakur was murdered in 1996, in what some claim was a "hit" put out by Notorious B.I.G.

Plenty of people would disagree with Mr. McWhorter's assumptions about the connection between rap and rudeness—but unfortunately, plenty more would agree. Even hip-hop fans admitted that rap music had taken a dark turn in the early 1980s when the "gangsta" style became popular.

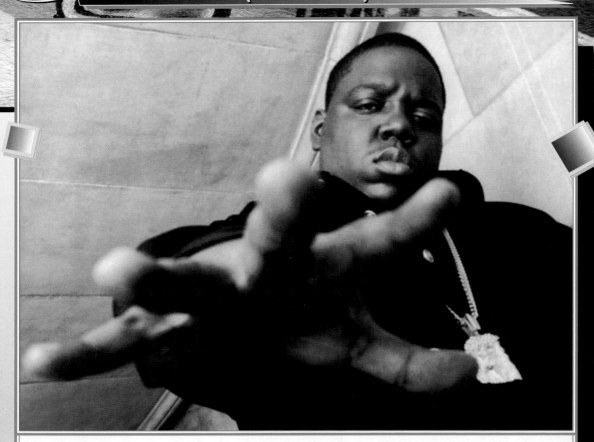

Though it was never proved, many believe that Notorious B.I.G. (also known as Biggie Smalls) was involved in Shakur's death. Six months after Shakur's death, Notorious B.I.G. himself was murdered in what many claim to be fallout from the East Coast–West Coast rap rivalry.

Gangsta rappers celebrated street warfare, drugs, and sexual promiscuity. Some people defended this style of rap, saying that it fell right in line with hip-hop's honesty; after all, violence, drugs, and sex *are* the reality in ghetto life. As Grandmaster Flash wrote in his 1982 hit "The Message": "You grow in the ghetto, living second rate/And your eyes will sing a song of deep hate."

Run-D.M.C. had never wanted to sing songs of hate. But even Run's brother, producer Russell Simmons, said that he despised the "soft, unaggressive music (and non-threatening images)" of black artists such as Michael Jackson or Luther Vandross. Other people, though, felt that hip-hop had gone too far when rappers like Tupac Shakur and Ice-T started rhyming about killing police. Other rappers—Schooly D and Jay-Z, for instance—produced songs that glorified the sexual **exploitation** and **objectification** of women.

Not only did rappers *talk* about violence—they crossed the line to actual violence. In 1995, Sean "P. Diddy" Combs, rap superstar,

Though he might not immediately come to mind when thinking about violence and hip-hop, Sean "P. Diddy" Combs (seen here in a 1998 photo) has had his share of criminal involvement. In 1999, while in a nightclub with Jennifer Lopez, he allegedly fired a gun.

producer, fashion mogul, and CEO of Bad Boy Records, was charged with possession of a deadly weapon. In 1999, Combs faced charges for assaulting a rival record executive. Later that year, police again charged him, this time for firing a gun at a nightclub in response to an insult; he injured three bystanders before he fled the scene. Combs was found not guilty, but his **protégé**, rapper Jamal "Shyne" Barrow, ended up being the one to go to prison for firing a gun.

Combs isn't the only allegedly violent hip-hop artist. Death Row Records producer Marion "Suge" Knight served five years for assault and federal weapons violations. 50 Cent was arrested for hiding assault weapons in his car. In 2000, at least five different fights broke out at the Source Hip-Hop Awards, and the final brawl was so big that it shut the ceremony down (ironically, right after a video tribute to slain rappers).

And yet many critics continue to admire hip-hop's brutal honesty. According to Russell Simmons, gangsta raps "teach listeners some-thing about the lives of the people who create them and remind them that these people exist." Even the National Council of Teachers of English recommends the use of hip-hop lyrics in urban public school classrooms, saying that "hip-hop can be used as a bridge linking the seemingly vast span between the streets and the world of academics."

After Jay's death, Run told Fox News:

❝When you think about rap music, you have to say, OK, this is the pain. This is the mirror of America. When you look at the mirror, all you're seeing is your-self. . . . [T]he poets are definitely just the voice of pain. . . . It's not so much the cursed words, it's the cursed ideas of America that we should be more worried about, not the [bad words], but more about what's going on to improve that problem in the hood.❞

Looking in the Mirror

Every story has two sides. That's certainly true when it comes to hip-hop music. People have good reasons for criticizing it—but other people have good reasons for defending it. Americans—especially white Americans sometimes—may not like facing what they see

Violence seems to follow Suge Knight, founder of Death Row Records. Though never charged, he has been implicated in the murders of Tupac Shakur and Notorious B.I.G. He has been in and out of prison, and in August 2005, Suge himself was shot and wounded.

when they look in hip-hop's mirror; they may not want to admit that they're looking at their own reflection, and so it's easier to condemn hip-hop than to face up to what's wrong in American society. On the other hand, it's hard to see how bad language and **misogyny** can make the world a better place. Words have power to create reality—and do we really want to create a reality where violence, money, and meaningless sex are the standards?

Some of the biggest names in hip-hop are facing these questions head on, including Run. They believe in hip-hop—and they're

Now that Run-D.M.C. was history, the Reverend Run went on with his life—his faith intact and his eyes on the greater good. He was ready to move on to a new chapter in his book of life.

convinced that it has power to do good. Folks like Mr. McWhorter may say, "Hip-hop creates nothing"—but Russell Simmons insists that "the coolest stuff about American culture—be it language, dress, or attitude—comes from the underclass. Always has and always will." Russell and Run are committed to making hip-hop a voice that speaks out for that underclass.

Keeping the Faith

In the early years of the twenty-first century, Run's life did a 180-degree turn. Jay was gone; Run-D.M.C. was gone; and hip-hop was facing some tough criticism. It was truly the end of an era. But Run held on to his faith.

Run's House Rule No. 7 goes like this:

> **"Problems occur to help direct you in life. Sometimes we only learn the value of something by losing it. Never believe it is over. . . . If your life isn't what you think it should be, don't give up."**

Run may not be making bestselling albums anymore—but he's doing something just as valuable with his life.

Family and giving back are important to Reverend Run. In this 2005 photo, Run poses with his wife and children at a benefit for the Rush Philanthropic Arts Foundation. Founded by Run and his brothers, the Rush Foundation funds art education programs for children.

Preaching the Faith

oday Run is a pastor at Zoe Ministries in Harlem; he is happily married to his second wife, Justine Jones; and he is the father of five children. Spreading the faith and taking care of his family are at the top of his list of priorities. But Run the rapper is still alive and well—and so is Run the businessman.

His current ventures include Run Athletics, a clothing company he launched in 2003. With his brother Russell, he co-owns Phat Fashions, and he is also president of Phat Farm Sneakers; in 2002, his new sneaker, the Phat Classic, sold over a million pairs. What's more, Run and Russell used funds from the sneaker to raise Americans' consciousness of the issue of **reparation** to black Americans for centuries of discrimination and slavery.

Making a Difference

Run believes that everything he does today is connected somehow to his faith. So whether he's standing in front of a church congregation or making money on his fashion line, he's always preaching the Word of God.

Run has released his first solo album, *Distortion*—but one of his newest ways of "preaching" is an MTV reality show called *Run's House*. The show features Run's real life, as well as that of his wife and his children. The show piloted in 2005, and did well enough in the ratings that it earned another season in 2006.

Run explained to NobodySmiling.com the connection between his faith and the reality show:

> **We grow up, we're fathers, we're family men. People don't see that side of rappers. Rap has come a long way and you see that on this reality show. . . . You'll see a lot of funny stuff, . . . you'll see a lot of me and my wife trying to hold the family together. . . . I can go to church and preach to the saved and that's good, but they're saved. Or I can . . . figure out how to catch everybody.**

Run figures that an MTV reality show gives him the chance to "catch" just about everyone. It also gives him the opportunity to show the world that hip-hop and violence don't have to be **synonomous**. He explained his thoughts further to NowOnTour:

> **There was man who [said], 'I can't hear nothing you say because your life is speaking so loud.' So, I'm going to let people see my life and I won't have to preach so loud. . . . The show opens up with a 'Word of Wisdom' where I write out a word of wisdom to people like Kid Rock, Serena Williams, LL Cool J, Puff Daddy. They show me getting in the tub in the morning writing it and then the show kind of intertwines during the day. You'll notice that my day is kind of connected to this 'Word of Wisdom' and at the end of the show, I'm . . . in the tub again.**

Acts of Charity

Run's life demonstrates that rappers can use their influence for good. He and his two brothers, Russell and Danny, work to help disadvantaged young people through the Rush Philanthropic Arts Foundation. The foundation brings together kids and art by funding art education

Reverend Run hasn't given up being a performer. In 2005, he released his first solo album, *Distortion*. He and his family are also featured on the MTV reality show *Run's House*, where viewers have the opportunity to see the family side of the hip-hop pioneer.

programs. It also offers a mentoring program that allows young people to hear the stories of artists who have risen above their circumstances.

Run knows that giving is an important piece of being a human being. He wrote in his memoir:

"Giving rightly is about purity of intention. Any time you get to the purity of yourself in any respect, you are fulfilling your purpose, forging your own unique path. Instead of walking through life as though a carrot is

Russell (left) and Reverend Run believe in helping young people. Here they celebrate the achievements of students during National Scholarship Month at Harlem's Young Women's Leadership School, the only all-girl public high school in New York City.

constantly dangling in front of your face, you become less calculating and attached to an outcome. You perform simply for the love of it. You give yourself to any task without regard for what you might get back. . . . Every time you're doing something that is beneficial not only to yourself but to everyone, you are contributing to society; you're giving of yourself.**"**

One of Russell Simmons' recent endeavors for society is the Hip-Hop Summit Action Network (HSAN), which he founded in 2001. Run has also gotten involved with this program, which, according to its Web site, "is dedicated to harnessing the cultural relevance of Hip-Hop music to serve as a **catalyst** for education **advocacy** and other societal concerns fundamental to the well-being of at-risk youth throughout the United States." HSAN's mission statement says that the organization is "united in the belief that Hip-Hop is an enormously influential agent for social change which must be responsibly and **proactively**

In 2001, Russell Simmons founded HSAN, and Reverend Run plays a big role in the organization. In 2004, he attended HSAN-sponsored events that encouraged young people—especially in black communities—to get educated about the issues, register, and vote.

Joey Simmons—Reverend Run—knows that a life can be changed. After all, he's experienced it himself. He believes that through faith and hard work, miracles can happen, and many lives change. With those lives changed for the better, the world will become a better place for all.

utilized to fight the war on poverty and injustice." Through HSAN, Run has lent his voice to a variety of good causes, including programs that work to encourage young African Americans to vote and get more involved with politics.

Run (and all the other HSAN members) have powerful intentions. According to the HSAN Web site, the organization is working to accomplish many worthwhile goals, such as: the total elimination of poverty; equal justice for all without discrimination based on race, color, ethnicity, nationality, gender, sexual orientation, age, creed or class; and freedom for all women, men, and children throughout the world.

These are truly lofty goals—but Run believes the world can be changed. He knows for a fact the power of faith to work miracles. Look inside yourself, he says, and you'll find what God wants you to do with your life to make a difference. "Everybody is sent to earth with a mission to do something," he says—and he's found his mission.

Run ends his memoir with his House Rule No. 13:

❝You are a star. Don't let anybody tell you otherwise. Everybody comes here with gifts. It takes time, but you will find your own.❞

1964 Joseph "Run" Simmons is born November 14 in Queens, New York.

1970s Hip-hop is born in the Bronx, New York.

1983 Run-D.M.C. signs with Prolific Records.

1984 Run-D.M.C. adopts their signature fashion style.

Run-D.M.C. becomes the first rap group to have an album go gold.

1985 Run-D.M.C. becomes the first rap group to have an album reach platinum status.

Run-D.M.C. performs at the Live Aid concert.

1986 Run-D.M.C. becomes the first rap group to earn a multi-platinum album.

Run-D.M.C. is the first rap group with a song to reach the top ten on *Billboard*'s Hot 100.

1987 Run-D.M.C. wins two *Soul Train* Music Awards.

1991 Run is accused of rape; the charges are later dropped.

1995 Run is ordained as a minister by Zoe Ministries.

2000 Run's book, *It's Like That: A Spiritual Memoir*, is published by St. Martin's Press.

2001 The Hip-Hop Summit Action Network, in which Run is very active, is founded.

2002 Run's Phat Classic sneaker sells more than one million pairs.

Run-D.M.C. becomes the first hip-hop group to be inducted into the Hollywood Rockwalk of Fame in Los Angeles, California.

Jam-Master Jay is murdered on October 30.

2003 Run launches Run Athletics, a clothing company.

2005 Run releases his first solo album.

Run's House premieres on MTV; it is renewed for 2006.

Discography
Run-D.M.C. Albums

1984	*Run-D.M.C.*
1985	*King of Rock*
1986	*Raising Hell*
1988	*Tougher Than Leather*
1990	*Back From Hell*
1991	*Together Forever: Greatest Hits 1983–1991*
1993	*Down With the King*
1999	*Crown Royal*
2002	*High Profile: The Original Rhymes Greatest Hits*
2003	*The Best of Run DMC Ultimate Run-D.M.C.*
2004	*Artist Collection: Run DMC*

Solo Albums

2005	*Distortion*

Selected Television Appearances

1985	*Live Aid*; *Graffiti Rock*
1986	*Abiyoyo*; *Reading Rainbow*; *Saturday Night Live*
1987	*Motown Merry Christmas*; *Showtime at the Apollo*
1988	*Yo! MTV Raps*
1989	*227*
1990	*Rapmania: The Roots of Rap*
1991	*The Howard Stern Show*
1992	*The Ben Stiller Show*
1998	*The Chris Rock Show*
2000	*Behind the Music*
2002	*Grounded for Life*; *Run-D.M.C. and Jam Master Jay: The Last Interview*; *The Weakest Link*
2004	*And You Don't Stop: 30 Years of Hip-Hop*
2005	*Run's House*; *Russell Simmons Presents Def Poetry*; *Sound Off*; *Weekends at the DL*; *Live with Regis and Kelly*; *The Tonight Show with Jay Leno*

Film

1985	*Krush Groove*
1988	*Tougher Than Leather*
1993	*Who's the Man?*
2002	*Red Dragon*

Video

1987	*Run-D.M.C.: The Video*
1989	*Wrestlemania V*
2000	*Run-D.M.C.: Together Forever—Greatest Hits 1983–2000*
2001	*MTV 20: Jams*
2002	*American Rap Stars*
	Through the Years of Hip Hop, Vol. 1: Graffiti
2003	*A Director's Journey: The Making of* Red Dragon
	Inside the Industry
	Lyricist Lounge: Hip Hop Video Classics

Awards

1987	Soul Train Music Awards: Best Rap Single; Best Rap Album
1988	Run-D.M.C. is nominated for a Grammy Award
2002	Run-D.M.C. is awarded the Kings of Hip-Hop Award from VH1
2003	VH-1 names Run-D.M.C. the greatest hip-hop artists
	VH-1 names "Walk This Way" one of the best songs of the past twenty-five years
	Rolling Stone puts *Raising Hell* and *Run-D.M.C.* on its list of the 500 Greatest Albums of All Time
2004	Reverend Run receives the Protégé Award and a lifetime achievement award for his mentoring activities from Zoe Ministries

Books

Adler, Bill. *Tougher Than Leather: The Rise of Run-DMC*. Los Angeles, Calif.: Consafos Press, 2002.

Ro, Ronin. *Raising Hell: The Reign, Ruin, and Redemption of Run-D.M.C. and Jam Master Jay*. New York: HarperCollins, 2005.

Simmons, Joseph, and Curtis L. Taylor. *It's Like That: A Spiritual Memoir*. New York: St. Martin's Press, 2000.

Magazines

"Black Celebrities Who Are Also Ministers." *Jet*, December 18. 1995.

Helhagar, Jeremy. "The Preacher's Life." *People*, July 29, 1996.

Warren, Tamara. "Hip-Hop Is a Hit." *AutoWeek*, January 30, 2006.

Willman, Chris. "Hear and Now." *Entertainment Weekly*, June 11, 1999.

Web Sites

"Dear Superstar: Reverend Run"
www.blender.com/guide/articles.aspx?id 1859

"Man of the House: Reverend Run"
www.newyorkmetro.com/nymetro/artstv/14710/index.html

Prophetic Minstrel
www.bishopjordan.com/school_prophecy/proph_minstrel/revrun.htm

Run's Rules
www.beliefnet.com/story/83/story_8309_1.html

advocacy—active verbal support for a cause or position.

affirmation—a positive statement.

blacklist—a list of people who are excluded from something.

catalyst—somebody or something that makes a change happen or brings about an event.

deacon—a layperson who assists a minister.

DJ—someone who plays recorded music for the entertainment of others; disc jockey.

dubbed—remixed records to bring some instruments into the foreground and causing others to echo.

epitome—a highly representative example of something.

exploitation—the unfair treatment or use of someone, usually for personal gain.

gold—signifying that a record has sold 500,000 copies.

improvised—made up without preparation.

memoir—someone's written account of his or her own life.

misogyny—the hatred of women as a group.

mixer—a machine that adjusts and combines various inputs to create a single output.

mogul—an important or powerful person.

objectification—the action of reducing someone that is complex and multifaceted to the status of a simple object.

ordained—officially and legally appointed as a minister, priest, or rabbi.

peerless—without equal.

platinum—a single that has sold one million copies, or an album or CD that has sold two million copies.

proactively—done in a manner of taking the initiative by acting rather than reacting to events.

progressive—forward-thinking.

protégé—a young person who receives help, guidance, and training from someone who is older and has more experience and influence.

reggae—popular music, originally from Jamaica, that combines elements of rock, calypso, and soul.

reparation—compensation for a wrong.

retaliation—the action of deliberately harming someone in response or revenge for a harm that person has committed.

synonymous—meaning the same or almost the same as something else.

testifying—talking to a group of people about one's own experiences.

Terrell Brown believes in the power of language to shape the world. He hopes to use his writing to encourage young people to become, in Reverend Run's words, "creative forces." Terrell lives in upstate New York with his family and five pet goats.

Picture Credits

page

2: Brian Prahl/Splash News
8: New Line Cinema/Photofest
11: Zuma Press Archive/NMI
12: Tina Paul/WENN
15: Zuma Press Archive/NMI
16: Deborah Feingold/Getty Images
18: NMI/Michelle Feng
21: Tsuni/iPhoto
23: AP Photo/Mark Lennihan
24: Warner Bros./Photofest
26: NMI/Michelle Feng
29: AP Photo/Marty Lederhandler
31: Marianne Armstrong/WENN
33: KRT/NMI

34: KRT/Richard Corkery
36: Tsuni/iPhoto
38: Reuters/Ethan Miller
41: Zuma Press/Toronto Star
42: NMI/Bad Boy Entertainment
43: UPI/Zio Petersen
45: KRT/Chuck Fadely
46: KRT/Tim Grant
48: INFGoff/infusny
51: NMI/Michelle Feng
52: PRNewsFoto/NMI
53: Marianne Armstrong/WENN
54: Adam Nemser-Photolink

Front cover: Reuters/Chip East
Back cover: Zuma Press/Robert Millard